PROJECT ECO-CITY

GLOBAL CITIES

PHILIP PARKER

Wayland

PROJECT ECO-CITY

Your Living Home
Your Wild Neighbourhood
Town Life
Global Cities

This book was prepared for Wayland (Publishers) Ltd by
Globe Education, Nantwich, Cheshire

Concept design and artwork by SPL Design

Cover picture: A kestrel in Colorado City.

First published in 1994 by
Wayland (Publishers) Ltd
61 Western Road, Hove
East Sussex, BN3 1JD, England

Printed and bound by
G. Canale & C. S. p. A., Turin

British Library Cataloguing in Publication Data
Parker, Philip
Global Cities. — (Project Eco-city Series)
I. Title II. Series
574.5268

ISBN 0 7502 1307 8

Picture acknowledgements
Colorific 32 (Stephen Shames)
Environmental Picture Library 7tl (Jimmy Holmes),18 (Martin Bond), 19t (Martin Bond),
19b (Charlotte MacPherson), 21 (Jimmy Holmes), 22 (Sheila Gray), 34 (Martin Bond)
Herbert Girardet 41; Images 11bl; Jimmy Holmes 23, 32
Lea Harrison 42; Mary Evans 6; Matrix 44
Oxford Scientific Films *cover* (Wendy Shattil & Bob Rozinski)
Oxfam 27 (Keith Bernstein)
Panos Pictures 5bl (Philip Wolmouth), 30 (Philip Wolmouth), 39t (D. Sansoni)
Science Photo Library 13 (Nasa), 38 (Sheila Terry), 45t (Peter Menzel), 45b (Roger Ressmeyer)
Still Pictures 5br, 8, 14tr, 14bl, 20t, 20b, 29tl, 29br, 31, 35, 36, 37, 43
Sue Cunningham 24tr, 27t
Tony Stone 4 (John Lawlor), 5t (David H Endersbee), 7tr (Suzanne & Nick Geary), 7bl (Doug Armand), 10,
15t (Ken Biggs), 24bl (John Starr), 25 (Rohan), 26 (Jenny Moulton), 33, 39b (Oliver Benn)
Zefa 11tr, 15b

Contents

Green or grey?

"God made the country,
and man made the town."

What would an alien visiting Earth think of this scene? Stone buildings growing to the sun with metal creatures crowding around them?

When these words were written by the English poet William Cowper two hundred years ago, only one person in ten lived in a city. For centuries, cities were thought of as places where nature had no place. They were important centres of trade, learning and money which were completely different from the countryside.

Yet isn't a city part of nature? Its crops may be concrete and asphalt, its creatures may be cars and lorries crawling along its roads. But it takes in food, coal, oil and gas from nature. It drains water from the region and gives back waste into the land, water and air. Cities grow, and sometimes even multiply when suburbs become large enough to be towns in their own right.

But cities are more than just buildings and cars. Our concern is also for the people who live and work in them and their quality of life.

Cities concentrate people and resources but whenever they grow above a certain size there are costs – in crime, pollution and roads clogged with traffic.

Today, five out of every ten people live in a town or city – and the number is rising. In the poorer, developing nations of the world, cities are growing so rapidly that housing and water supplies cannot keep up. In the richer industrial countries, cities use more resources and create more pollution, but they are growing more slowly – some such as London are actually losing people as they move to smaller towns in search of a better life away from the traffic jams and pollution. Few cities seem to be giving their citizens a truly good quality of life. But much can be done to improve life in cities and make them far less consuming and polluting of nature – more 'green' and less grey.

▲ Cities squeeze people, shops, offices and transport into small areas.

▲ Cities are the centres for a country's markets and businesses.

◄ For all their problems cities are some of the most exciting places.

City beginnings

People have been building cities for thousands of years. But only recently have cities become the home of half the human race.

When humans first lived on the Earth, they did not live in one place. They wandered in groups, gathering plants for food and hunting animals. Then around 12,000 years ago, humans discovered how to grow food by sowing seeds and tending plants. This meant staying in one place and so the first small settlements were built.

Florence's trading links with other countries helped to make it one of the wealthiest cities of Europe by the seventeenth century.

Around 10,000 years ago some of these settlements had grown into the first towns. In these early towns, enough food could be produced to feed specialist workers – soldiers, craftspeople, merchants and rulers, for example – as well as farmers.

As the first towns prospered and began trading together, some grew into cities. Along the Tigris and Euphrates rivers in present day Iraq, the first big cities grew 6,000 years ago. In regions of India, Egypt and China other cities grew and flourished. By AD 100 the then biggest city in the world, Rome, was home to 650,000 people and the centre of a vast empire ruling much of Europe and North Africa.

For most of history, wood was the major fuel. Without it, buildings and ships could not be built and the powering of early industries would have been impossible. The shift to the more plentiful coal as a fuel was very important. Coal powered the Industrial Revolution – a time when new machines and factories were created. People began to leave the farms to work in the growing towns. In 1800 at the start of the Industrial Revolution, there were only 25 cities with a population larger than 200,000 people. Yet 100 years later, there were almost 150 of them.

▲ The remains of Mohenjodaro – a city
which flourished 4,500 years ago
in present-day Pakistan.

▲ Paris has been a major
city for 2,000 years.

◄ New York was founded
by settlers from Europe
in the seventeenth century.
Today it is one of the world's
financial centres.

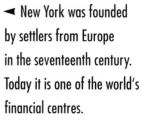

Megacities

In 1950, only 29 per cent of the world's people lived in a town or city. Today, almost half of all people are in 'urban' areas. There are now 14 megacities with more than 10 million people each. Ten of these are in the poorer, developing world. In 1950 the developing world had none.

The future is even more urban. The number of people in towns and cities is increasing by 80 million a year – that's 10 cities the size of London or Moscow. By the year 2025 probably two out of every three people will live in a town or city.

Urban areas swell not just with their own population increase but by the movement of people from the country. Every day about 75,000 people around the world stream into cities from the countryside looking for work and a place to live. Most of them end up building their own homes in shanty towns. Such 'home-made' settlements house as much as three-quarters of the population of some cities, for example Calcutta.

Large cities demand huge amounts of water, food, shelter and transport, but in poor shanty towns conditions can be bad. City authorities in many countries cannot provide new services at the speed with which their cities expand. In the developing nations about 20 per cent of urban residents do not have safe drinking water. In country areas 40 per cent do not have clean water. Adequate toilet and sewage facilities are even harder to find. One-third of developing world city people do not have these, compared to 80 per cent of the country population. This means that around the world 270 million people still don't have safe water to drink, and 470 million do not have adequate sanitation in cities.

Mexico City is likely to be home to 25 million people by the year 2000. Up to one-third may be living in shanty houses.

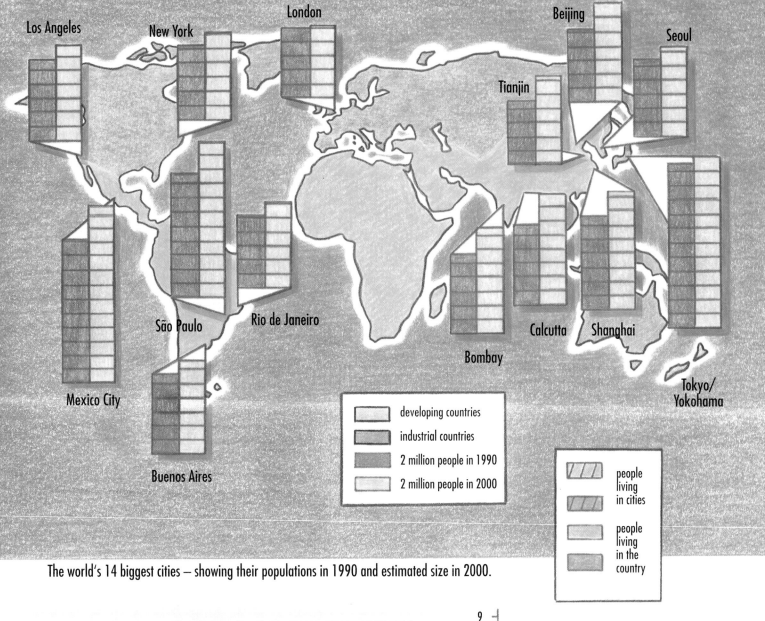

The world's 14 biggest cities – showing their populations in 1990 and estimated size in 2000.

Map labels: Los Angeles, New York, London, Beijing, Seoul, Tianjin, Mexico City, São Paulo, Rio de Janeiro, Buenos Aires, Bombay, Calcutta, Shanghai, Tokyo/Yokohama

Legend:
- developing countries
- industrial countries
- 2 million people in 1990
- 2 million people in 2000

- people living in cities
- people living in the country

DID YOU KNOW?

A world of cities

Of the world's 5,500 million people, half are urban. In industrial countries, around three-quarters of the people live in towns or cities. In developing countries, about 40 per cent are urban. Cities are found in every country. The most northerly capital city is Reykjavik in Iceland, the most southerly is Wellington in New Zealand. The highest city in the world is Lhasa, 3,684 m up in the Tibetan mountains.

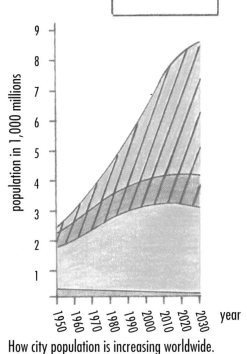

How city population is increasing worldwide.

Consuming cities

Cities can be troubled places – but their difficulties do not remain within their borders, they can affect the whole world.

Land in cities is put to different uses. The city centre is densely built up with the offices of government and business. The price of land is high and people and industry move outward. Homes and recreational areas are further from the centre and usually less built up, but sprawl over the land is eating up the countryside. The population of New York has increased by just 5 per cent in the last 25 years, but its area has grown by more than half.

The city competes for land with farms and forests. Cities are usually built on good farmland and as they grow they push the farms on to less suitable lands. The risk of soil erosion, where soil gets blown or washed away, increases. At the same time, cities demand that the farms produce more food to feed their people. Cities in poor nations use up forests – mostly for fuel. Around cities like Nairobi in Kenya and Delhi in India, there are no forests left for many kilometres. Most of Delhi's firewood is brought by train from forests 700 km away.

The city sprawl goes on.

The Australian city of Sydney grew up around its harbour – into which building materials could be brought and through which the growing city could trade. ➤

◄ Millions of people travel into cities every day in search of jobs and better working conditions.

Although richer nations do not use trees for fuel, they use them for building and for paper. The precious rain forests of the tropics are being cut, in part to supply city people with fine wood, and the ancient forests of northern Canada are felled to provide the pulp to make paper for Europe and North America. Each minute, five old Canadian trees fall, some of them 1,000 years old, and along with them the habitats for wildlife.

As well as materials, cities also drain the countryside of minds! Millions of people leave the countryside for the city, draining rural areas of much-needed brain-power.

Powering cities

When astronauts in space pass over the dark side of the Earth they are still able to see the world's cities. Lights from buildings and streets shine so brightly that cities and towns can be seen from space as dots of light. The cities are using huge amounts of electricity to make them so visible from the sky.

Every day, millions of tonnes of fuel are burned to provide energy for the Earth's people. Most of this fuel is burned for cities. Most of the world's electricity comes from burning coal, oil and natural gas. These 'fossil fuels' are burned in power stations to provide the energy to create electricity. But these fuels also release waste gases into the air.

Cities are responsible for most of the pollution which could lead to climate change – and a rise in sea levels which could flood the cities shown below. The richer industrial cities produce the most 'greenhouse' gases shown by the plumes of smoke.

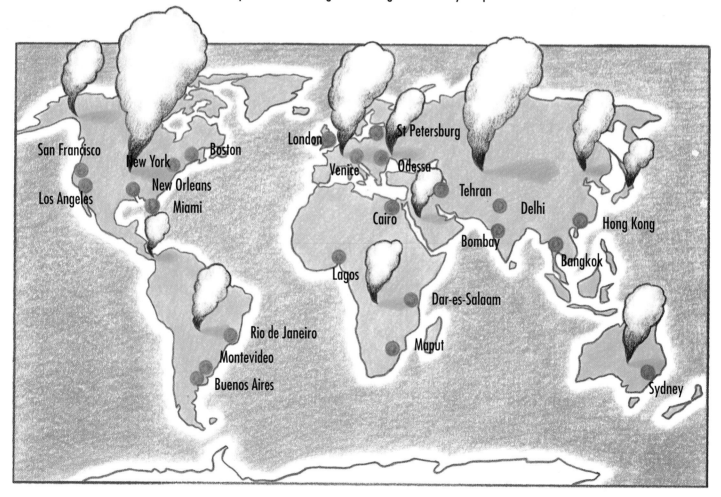

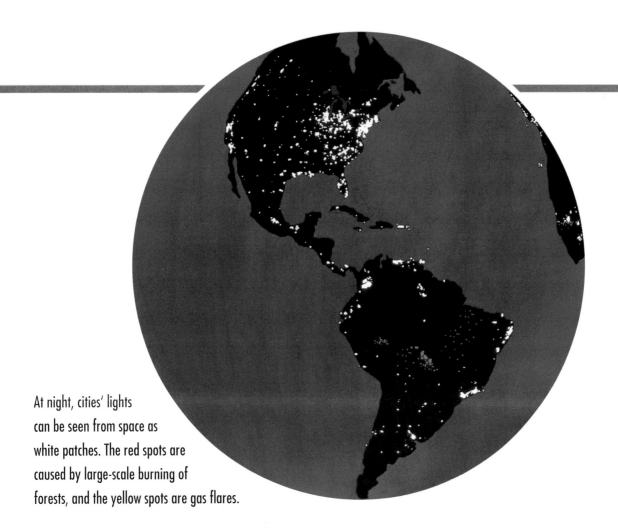

At night, cities' lights can be seen from space as white patches. The red spots are caused by large-scale burning of forests, and the yellow spots are gas flares.

The world's 550 million cars, lorries and buses also burn fossil fuel and produce waste gases. Most of these vehicles are concentrated in cities.

Some of the gases released when fossil fuels are burned are known as greenhouse gases. These can trap heat in the atmosphere and warm the Earth – rather like the glass in a greenhouse. Since the Industrial Revolution and the use of fossil fuels, the amount of carbon dioxide – the main greenhouse gas – has increased by a quarter. The amount of another greenhouse gas, methane, has doubled. Average world temperatures have increased by 0·5 °C. This may seem very little, but many of the scientists who study the climate believe that the warming is increasing. Climate change could lead to major changes in the weather affecting the growing of food. It could also melt ice in the Arctic and other places, adding water to the oceans and making sea levels rise.

Many of the world's biggest cities are built on coasts or in low-lying river valleys. One-third of world's people live within 65 km of the sea. They could all be seriously affected by floods – perhaps within one hundred years. Food supplies would also be threatened. Cities would be the victim of climate change, as well as the chief cause. But cities can also take action to help avoid possible disaster.

Car chaos

Cities are powered mostly by coal (for electricity) and oil (for transport). Perhaps the car has changed the face of the Earth more than any other human invention. One new car leaves a production line somewhere in the world every second.

On average, one-third of a city's area is devoted to vehicles – roads, garages, parking lots. Cities that have been built or grown since the invention of the car have been shaped by it.

Rush hour – the same in cities the world over, such as here in Manila.

The pollution from traffic is a major health problem everywhere.

Los Angeles, for example, has sprawling suburbs and long freeways – the planners assumed all people would have cars. Two-thirds of Los Angeles is given over to cars. But by the year 2000 the average speed of a car in Los Angeles is expected to be as low as 25 kph because of traffic congestion. The building of roads also destroys countryside important for wildlife, and mining the rocks and gravel needed creates huge quarries eating into more land.

Cars burn oil (as petrol), a precious resource which will one day run out. Two-thirds of the oil burned in the USA each year is burned in cars. In Europe it is half.

Burning petrol creates pollution. Lead, added to much of the petrol that is used, is given out in car exhausts and can cause damage to children's brains. Other chemicals can give rise to smogs which can cause illnesses. Burning petrol in car engines is also a major source of the greenhouse gas, carbon dioxide.

Cars also kill – about 250,000 people a year are killed in road accidents, most of which happen in towns and cities.

About 1·5 per cent of the world's 550 million cars are squeezed into one city, Los Angeles – home to 0·2 per cent of the world's people.

CALIFORNIA'S NEW CARS

The 10·5 million people of Los Angeles suffer the worst air pollution in the USA; the main problem is the 8 million cars. Los Angeles has the highest number of vehicles per person in the world and they are the main cause of the smogs which plague the city. To tackle the problem, California now has some of the strongest laws on air pollution in the world. By the year 2003, for example, the polluting gases produced by cars must be drastically cut. One-tenth of all cars sold must run on fuels other than petrol – such as electricity or natural gas. Some scientists worry that even this will not be enough to improve the air as the number of cars on the roads increases.

The search for no, or low, pollution cars continues. This car runs on hydrogen – a possible fuel of the future. Already, one million cars worldwide run on natural gas, and there are thousands of electric cars.

Generation game

How we generate and use energy is a key to reducing cities' consumption of resources and lowering pollution levels.

Coal and oil contain sulphur which is released when the fuels are burned. The sulphur, and other chemicals, mix with the moisture in the air and form an acid rain which is capable of making lakes lifeless and damaging forests. Many new power stations are fitted with filters to greatly reduce the amount of the acid-rain making chemicals released. But this makes the power station less efficient which means that more coal has to be burned to make the same amount of electricity as before.

Fossil fuel power stations are very wasteful. Only about 40 per cent of the energy in the fuel becomes useful energy at home.

A combined heat and power station creates electricity — but also provides hot water for a town or neighbourhood.

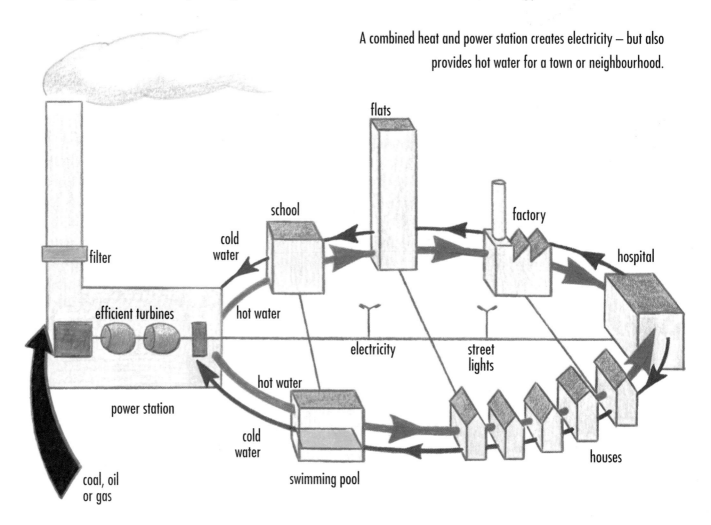

The other 60 per cent is lost as heat through cooling towers and when the electricity runs through cables to towns. Yet there are ways of improving efficiency – so less fuel is burned and less pollution is created.

The waste heat that is lost from power stations can be saved and piped directly to homes and industry. A town's power station generates the electricity but the waste hot water can be pumped through insulated pipes around the town to warm schools factories, swimming pools, hospitals and other buildings.

About 80 per cent of the energy stored in the fuel is then used – so far less fossil fuel is needed. These combined heat and power (CHP) systems are already in use in hundreds of cities. In Helsinki – the capital city of Finland – 80 per cent of homes are heated by CHP, and in Holland 800 mini-CHPs provide heat and hot water to local neighbourhoods.

RUN A SCHOOL ECO-AUDIT

Every time you switch on a light, you use electricity. But energy is also used to make our everyday things like pencils, paper and books. Your school uses a lot of energy through the materials it uses up. Investigate this with an audit. Start in your classroom. Get everyone to fill in a survey – a few ideas are shown below. Make graphs or pie-charts of the results.

How many text and reading books do you have – are any labelled as being made of recycled paper? Is broken equipment thrown away, repaired or used for something else?

Ask other classes to run the audit giving them copies of the survey. Compare and add up all the results to give an idea of how much paper and books are used by the students.

Invent a new list for teachers and other school staff. For example, in the school kitchen are the plates and cups reusable or are they plastic and disposable? What happens to the food waste – is it composted or binned? Are paper towels and toilet paper made from recycled material? Is there a recycling scheme to collect waste paper and cardboard, cans and glass bottles?

Writing
> I use ___ throwaway pens/refillable pens/no pens
> I write on ___ pages of paper a day
> They are labelled/not labelled *recycled paper*
> I use___ pages of computer paper a day

Saving paper
> I write on one side/both sides of a piece of paper
> I write small/large

Numbers
> I use a battery/solar powered calculator/none

Travel
> I get to school by walking/cycling/bus/car

Home energy saving

When it is cold outside, the warmth in your home leaks away and the heating system needs to work hard to replace it. More than half the energy we use at home is to provide heating or air-conditioning and up to half of that is wasted. In a town, about one-third of all energy is used in people's homes. If some of this could be saved then the greenhouse and acid rain gases being produced at power stations would be reduced.

About 15 per cent of the heat lost from a house seeps through the gaps around window frames and doors. Sealing these gaps saves energy for little cost. The windows also allow heat to escape. Double glazing reduces this, but so do thick curtains. The warmest air in a house rises to the ceiling. Here the warmth seeps upstairs or into the attic where it can escape. A thick 15 cm layer of insulation in the loft stops most of this heat floating away.

In homes heated by radiators, about one-sixth of the heat is wasted as the radiators warm the walls behind them. Aluminium foil behind the radiators will reflect the heat back. Heat escapes through walls as much as through double glazed windows but can be reduced by filling the space inside the walls with insulation. This is expensive but saves its cost in energy in 3 or 4 years.

Best of all, it is important not to waste energy. Switch off lights in rooms not in use and use lids on saucepans to keep the heat in. Light bulbs turn only 10 per cent of the electricity into light – the rest is wasted as heat. Low energy fluorescent bulbs use just a quarter of the electricity ordinary bulbs need – and last about 10 times longer – which saves on the energy needed to make them.

Filling the gap between walls dramatically reduces heat loss.

A house can lose about 15 per cent of its heat through the roof – insulation cuts this down.

In our homes there are energy-eating machines. Go on an energy-eater hunt. Some machines have big appetites. Look for heaters, lights, hot water taps, cookers, Hoovers and TVs. Anything with an electric motor is a big energy-eater. How many motors are there in your kitchen? Look for air extractors, blenders and food mixers, washing and drying machines, dishwashers. Fridges and freezers are driven by motors. There are eight motors in the average US kitchen. How many are there in yours? How many of them are essential?

Electricity shops and showrooms should be able to tell you about energy-efficient products – some are labelled to show how much energy they use.

Now look for the hidden energy eaters. Energy is used to make metal, glass, plastic, paint, bricks, paper, carpets and the packaging we buy our food in. How many can you find?

Energy saving fluorescent lights use just a quarter of the electricity ordinary bulbs need – and last about 10 times longer.

Cleaner energy

Most of our energy comes from burning fossil fuels – as well as from nuclear power. These sources create serious pollution problems and will one day be used up. There are cleaner energy sources which are not so damaging to the environment. Natural, or renewable, energy sources are continually replaced such as the power of the sun, the waves and the wind.

Using natural energy is not new. Windmills were invented about 2,500 years ago, but in the last ten years more than 20,000 large wind-turbines have been built around the world, and another 40,000 are planned over the next 15 years. Most wind turbines are in California where they supply one per cent of the state's electricity – enough to provide power for 900,000 people.

If electric cables do not already run near a house, it is cheaper to buy and fit solar cells to make a home's electricity.

The old and the new ways of providing power in the Netherlands.

Half of all our energy needs are for heat. Solar collectors gather and store the sun's energy to heat water and buildings. In Tokyo more than 1·5 million solar collectors provide hot water and in Israel two-thirds of homes have them.

Solar energy can power a generator or be turned into electricity in 'solar cells'. These cells are expensive to make but the cost is only one-tenth of ten years ago and is still falling. In Norway, 50,000 homes have solar cells fitted on roofs and walls. A Japanese scientist has suggested that energy needs in 2000 might be met by solar cells covering just 4 per cent of the world's deserts.

Deep below the ground, the Earth is very hot. Many countries are using this heat to provide energy. In certain places a hole of several kilometres deep is drilled and cold water pumped down to the hot rocks. The heated water or steam is then pumped back and used to warm buildings or power a turbine for electricity. The Philippines makes 14 per cent of its electricity this way.

Boiling water with a solar kettle in Tibet. Solar cookers were invented 200 years ago. In the USA there are about 10,000 in use.

MAKE A SOLAR SAUSAGE COOKER

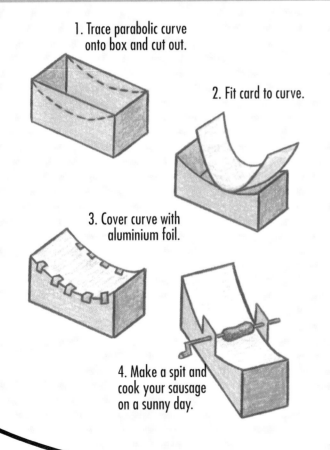

1. Trace parabolic curve onto box and cut out.

2. Fit card to curve.

3. Cover curve with aluminium foil.

4. Make a spit and cook your sausage on a sunny day.

Trace the 'parabolic' curve on to the sides of a narrow box and carefully cut out the curves.

Cut a piece of thin card so it fits exactly into the curved top. Fix with tape. Glue a length of aluminium foil to it – shiny side out. Smooth out any wrinkles.

Tape a piece of cardboard to each side of the box at the centre. Mark each card 15 cm above the centre of the curve. Make holes here for the spit – a piece of wire coat hanger.

Choose a bright warm day, put a sausage lengthwise on the spit and face the cooker into the sun. Time how long it takes for any changes to happen. It could take more than an hour to cook a sausage.

template for parabolic curve

Ask an adult to check if the food is cooked – do not eat it if you are in any doubt.

Reduce, reuse, recycle

Up to 70 per cent of the rubbish in a waste bin can be recycled. Most German homes have at least four bins – grey for rubbish that will be dumped, green for paper, blue for food and yellow for anything else such as tins. Glass is collected separately. Germany has new laws to improve recycling. Manufacturers and shops must now take back packaging from their customers for reuse and recycling.

Recycling saves raw materials and energy. Reuse is even more effective. Old clothes, toys and books can be sold in special shops. In Germany more than 80 per cent of drinks sold in shops are in refillable containers. Repairing things rather than throwing them out and buying new ones also saves on the disposal of the old and the energy needs to create the new.

Urban Ore is a company in the USA that collects anything from old furniture to computers, repairs them and sells them on to those in need.

But even more effective than reusing is reducing. Up to two-thirds of all waste from the home is packaging. We pay for the packaging three times. Once when it is bought, again when it is collected as refuse and finally in damage to the environment when the refuse is dumped or burned. So, take a bag with you when shopping. Large economy size packets and bottles of goods use less packaging than smaller ones. Everything we buy has some effect on the environment. If enough people refuse to buy over-packaged items, manufacturers may finally decide to change and reduce the packaging around their goods.

Doorstep collections of materials for recycling is best. Many people drive to recycling centres which can use up more energy and make more pollution than the recycling can save.

Chopping cans in Phnom Penh, Cambodia, to separate the more valuable aluminium from the steel. The woman then sells the metals to scrap merchants.

MAKE YOUR OWN RECYCLED PAPER

Make two identical frames from eight bits of wood each about 30 cm long. Use waterproof glue and nails. Stretch fine mesh over one frame and fix with drawing pins making a sieve. Put the empty frame on top of the sieve.

30 cm

frames

30 cm

Make pulp by tearing about 30 sheets of used computer or photocopier paper into small squares and soaking overnight in water. Take a handful of wet paper and crush with a potato masher. Put the pulp into a large bowl of warm water.

mesh

30 cm

30 cm

Dip the sieve and frame in the mix. Shake to get an even layer of pulp. Lift out and drain. Place the sieve, paper side down, onto a piece of kitchen cloth. Gently lift the sieve leaving the paper behind on the cloth. Put more kitchen cloth on top of the paper. Put a board on top of this and press out the water.

frames after dipping in pulp mixture

pulp

water is squeezed out

paper is turned out on kitchen paper

pulp balls

allow water to drain

Leave the recycled paper in a warm place to dry before trimming. Repeat the process again to make more paper.

City festivals

Cities create! Nowhere else is there such a mix of peoples living, working and playing together!

Cities attract people and often absorb different cultures from around the world. Does your city have a Chinatown, a Little Italy or other district with people originally from another country? People are forever on the move, from countryside to the city, and from one country to another. In the USA, for example, more than 25 major languages are spoken. Into the cities of the USA come people from Asia, Latin America and the Caribbean. Seven million people have moved from Central America to the USA in the past 20 years. There are more Mexicans in Los Angeles than in any other city in the world except Mexico City. The most widely used language after English is Spanish; more than 17 million people speak Spanish as

Celebrating together in London's yearly Notting Hill carnival.

their main language. Miami is already half Spanish-speaking. Around 15 per cent of all Americans speak a language other than English as their first language. In the city of London, nearly 200 different languages can be heard. After English, Turkish and Chinese are the most common.

For several days every February normal life in Rio de Janeiro, Brazil, stops to make way for the parade.

This diversity of peoples is celebrated in festivals and carnivals the world over. In Brazil, the annual February parade in Rio de Janeiro first started 150 years ago. Hundreds of thousands of people following the musicians and dancers block the streets.

In London's Notting Hill district a carnival was first held in 1967 – it was intended to bring people together from different cultures. Today this annual event draws tens of thousands of people and is copied in cities throughout Britain.

Our cities have also always been centres of religion. Temples, mosques and cathedrals are among the most important and central buildings in a city. Rome, Mecca and Jerusalem are the religious capitals for three of the world's largest religions.

Jerusalem – the ancient religious centre for Jewish, Christian and Muslim people.

DID YOU KNOW?

Plants and people

As people have travelled around the world, they have taken plants with them from country to country. Azaleas, rhododendrons and maple trees originally came from China and Japan. Buddleia was first found in China, and pineapple weed comes from north-east Asia. Red-hot pokers were brought from Africa and pampas grass from South America. Herbs such as rosemary and lavender originally came from the Mediterranean.

Street art

Cities have long been centres for art. The sculptures, buildings and plays created in the Athens of the Ancient Greeks have influenced people for more than 2,000 years. The Italian city of Florence grew in the fifteenth century because of its trade with other cities. It was the leading city of the Renaissance and the home of Leonardo da Vinci.

Today, cities still influence culture. City authorities pay artists to create works of art in their cities and sculptures are often seen either of famous city people or modern works. Art can even help to reverse a city's decline. Over the past ten years Glasgow, Scotland's second biggest city, has been transformed into a leading city of the arts. Its Mayfest held every year is one of Europe's most important arts festivals.

Graffiti artists, or 'graffers' often work in secret at night. They cover walls, trains and railway stations with brightly coloured murals with spray paint or pen. Many also scrawl their signature, or 'tag', over walls. The London underground train system spends £2 million a year cleaning off graffiti and is now protecting its trains in non-stick paint on which spray paint won't stay. In London around 70 graffiti artists are active. Their activities are a crime in Britain, but in the USA graffiti is often thought of as art. It can even be seen in art galleries. Jean Michel Basquint was a graffiti artist whose paintings on scrap metal and other dumped material sells for $100,000 each. So is graffiti ugly and expensive vandalism, or is it a way of brightening a grey wall with art?

Sometimes graffiti is organized. In Britain, The Freeform Arts Trust helps people decorate building hoardings and ugly walls with murals and mosaics, allowing ordinary people the chance to change their environment.

A New York City scene – where graffiti was invented.

A colourful mural painted on a wall in Brazil.

To find junk you must search around. Always sort through rubbish with rubber gloves, and take care of sharp objects. Start with old packaging and paper from your bin, but look for old sticks, pebbles – anything.

Make a sculpture out of the materials you have collected. Glue the pieces together to make, perhaps, a recycling monster, a tree or an animal (how about a town fox?). Try to create a musical instrument – something that can be hit with a stick, or with strings to pluck.

Try making a poster – think of a suitable subject, for example a poster asking people to recycle their rubbish. On a large sheet of paper or card, arrange and glue the junk into position.

In your city there may be boardings or temporary walls put across building sites. You might be able to find the owner of the site or the company doing the building (check the boarding for a poster giving their name, address or phone number). Contact them and see if they would allow you and your friends to paint a mural on the boarding.

All over the world, children, like this boy in Mozambique, make toys from waste material.

City lights

Although a human invention, a city can be a harsh place for people to live in.

In the developing world especially, more and more people are moving to the cities. People leave the countryside because they think they will have a better life in the city. In the country, land to farm and jobs may be scarce but city jobs pay better. The money from one city job can support a whole family in the country, and in cities there are more schools, hospitals and doctors.

The families who arrive in the city often face disappointment. If they are poor, they cannot afford housing and so they find other ways to shelter. In dozens of developing countries, it is poor families who are making cities grow in new directions. In these cities about three-quarters of all new housing is built by the poor people themselves in shanty towns. In fact, two-thirds of all the world's houses were built by the people who live in them. In a city such as Bangkok up to one million people live in home-made houses. In Calcutta, 75 per cent of the population live this way.

These shanty towns sprawl around the city but many of their streets are not connected to the city's clean water and sewage systems. Up to one third of the people may have no work, and those that do work might travel long distances into the city on overcrowded buses or trains, working long hours for low pay.

Areas around cities where shanty towns can be built are often dangerous. The steep hillsides around Rio de Janeiro, for example, are home to several shanty towns. In 1988, severe rain caused floods which ran down the hillside, washing away homes and killing hundreds of people. Other shanty towns are built alongside rivers that fill with the city's sewage and cause health problems.

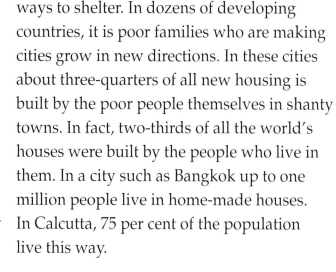

This family built their own home in Khulna, Bangladesh.

Rosinha is the biggest shanty town in South America, housing 250,000 people on the steep hillsides above Rio de Janeiro, a city where one in five people live in a shanty town. All the houses were built by the families who live in them. They have also built health clinics, shops and meeting halls. Three-quarters of the homes are made of brick, and some are three storeys high. Only the poorest live in wooden shacks.

▲ Rosinha is not a new shanty town – people built the first houses there 150 years ago.

◄ Rosinha is a real town with schools and health centres.

The people of Rosinha have persuaded the city authorities to connect most of the houses at the bottom of the hill to Rio's water and sewage systems. But the poorer houses higher up the hill still pour sewage into the gutters. Three-quarters of the houses are also supplied with electricity. Several homes share a meter and are connected up to the city's electricity supply. The people of Rosinha are now working with city officials to build better drains and sewers, organize the collection of rubbish and lay pipes to provide the poorest neighbourhoods with clean water.

Street life

As well as the hazards of life in shanty towns, many poor people in cities are forced to live and work on the streets. These are the poorest of the poor and the new arrivals who have no money to pay for shelter in cities where already there is not enough housing for people in need.

Homeless people can be found in almost every city. Perhaps as many as 100 million people in the world are homeless. In Calcutta, India, for example, as many as 600,000 people live on the streets. Most of these 'pavement dwellers' live near the train lines. It is easiest to travel in and out of the city in search of work along the tracks, and they can also sell food to people travelling on the trains.

In cities great wealth can be found next to enormous poverty. An empty area of 2,000 hectares in Bombay is owned by just one family. This is enough space to house all the city's shanty town and pavement dwellers. Where land prices are high, thousands of people sleep in the open, or build shelters from old sacks and poles on streets and under bridges.

One of the thousands of homeless people in London, sleeping rough in a doorway.

Street children at work in a city park in Curitiba, Brazil.

Brazil in South America has the highest number of street children of any country in the world; there are believed to be seven million children living and working on the streets of the cities. Some do have shelters and homes to return to at night but all of them scratch a living by cleaning car windscreens, shoe-shining, selling matches or items they have made from scrap, or by begging.

Even in rich cities, homelessness is a problem. People without money or work find it so difficult to get somewhere to live that they sometimes end up living on the streets. There are believed to be up to 40,000 homeless people on the streets of Paris. Some are lucky enough to have beds in hostels for the night, but they must spend their days in the city, often begging for money. In Paris more than 100,000 buildings are empty. Could some of these buildings be opened to provide shelter – or even homes – for the homeless?

DID YOU KNOW?

Voice in the street

In Europe and the USA many homeless people are helped by the sale of 'street magazines'. In London, *The Big Issue* is produced twice a month. Homeless people can buy copies for 30p each, but then sell them on the streets for 60p. About 700 homeless people sell 100,000 copies of the magazine weekly. In New York, street people sell *Street News*. Across Europe similar magazines are sold – in total about one million a month.

Quality of life

To walk along many streets is to brave noise, smog and traffic. For most town people the quality of the environment has altered a great deal in the last 30 years. Traffic and road building have swallowed up huge areas of land, changing the way people live and their ideas about what town life should be.

Local shops have given way to big supermarkets which are sometimes on the edge of town, making life more difficult for those without cars, including children. Towns have been designed for cars, not children, older people or people with disabilities who all struggle with busy roads.

We don't often think of noise as pollution – but it is when it happens in the wrong place at the wrong time. The roar of motorbikes or cars in the middle of the night, noisy neighbours and barking dogs are the main reasons why 55,000 British people complain to their local authorities each year. People living near airports can suffer particularly badly when jets roar overhead as they take off or land.

Many people feel very lonely in cities – often there is little sense of community. Cars have helped to make this worse. In San Francisco scientists made a survey of people living in streets in similar areas. They found that the people who lived on streets with the lightest traffic had three times as many friends as those who lived on streets with heavy traffic.

Sometimes cities can seem lonely, frightening places.

The scientists found that on the quiet streets people stop and talk and children play on the pavements. But the busy streets are no more than roads linking homes to the outside world. Cars take over the roads and their noise and dirt mean that people do not linger on the pavements. They abandon their front gardens and even their front rooms because of the noise on the busiest streets.

Can those living near airports ever get used to the noise?

QUALITY OF LIFE SURVEY

What do people think about their local environment? Write a series of questions and go out on the street to interview people. You don't need 'experts' – interview older people, children, police, rubbish collectors.

Rehearse with a friend before you interview and plan what to say. Go with a friend and wear a badge or sticker with your name and saying 'Quality of life survey' so people know what you are doing.

You could record your interviews on tape, along with the age of the person and whether they are male or female.

1. Do you live or work in this neighbourhood?
   If yes, why did you choose here?
   If no, what brings you here?

2. Do you think the streets are clean enough?

3. Are there parts of the neighbourhood you don't like to visit?

4. Has the area changed since you've been here - for better or worse?

5. What do you like about the neighbourhood?

6. What do you dislike?

7. Want changes do you think would improve the area?

8. Would you like more money to be spent on improving the neighbourhood, even if this means higher bills?

Getting around

Travelling around cities can be fun – it can also be frustrating. New ideas are making cities easier to navigate in.

Between 1888 and 1917 some 72,000 km of streetcar (tram) lines were built in US cities. Los Angeles had an excellent system but this was abandoned in favour of the car. In the past 30 years, the number of cars on US roads has doubled while traffic delays have increased three times. Another doubling of traffic is expected over the next 30 years.

Years ago, people travelled from homes in the suburbs to work in the middle of town; transport systems followed these routes. Today, two-thirds of US workers travel from suburb to suburb to work. Rail lines don't usually follow this path, and so 87 per cent of US workers drive their cars to work. Only 5 per cent use public transport.

Cities are again looking to public transport to stop the pollution and clogging of roads. Amsterdam in The Netherlands has one of the best transport systems of any city. Visitors arrive by train at the centre and can travel anywhere in the city centre by the frequent trams. Bus and bike lanes lead out to the suburbs. Following this example, the British industrial cities of Manchester and Sheffield have brought back trams after 50 years in which the roads were dominated more and more by cars.

Curitiba in Brazil has 1·6 million people. It has tripled in size in just 25 years. City officials decided to build the best public bus system they could. The city centre is closed to cars and high speed buses flow along all the main roads – including the biggest bus in the world which carries 270 people.

One of the new electric trams in the centre of Manchester, UK.

More people own cars in Curitiba than in any other city in Brazil – but they use them less because of the excellent bus services.

Choose a main road to investigate traffic. Make a table like the one below to record the number of vehicles you see heading into town during a 15 minute period. Put a tick for each vehicle you see and add up the ticks at the end. Start about 3 or 4 km from the town centre. Then repeat the test 0·5 km from the centre of town.

What kind of vehicle is most common? Where is there most traffic – and why? Is it easy for people to cross the road safely? How safe is it to cycle? What could be done to make the road safer for pedestrians and cyclists?

Always be very careful of traffic when working near roads.

Kind of vehicle	Number of vehicles seen in 15 minutes	
	3 km from centre	0·5 km from centre
cars		
buses		
vans and lorries		
motorbikes		
bicycles		

Bike to the future

In 1991, six New York cyclists were in court for stopping traffic on the city's Queensboro Bridge. The QB6 – as they became known – were protesting at the closing of a cycle lane on the bridge. Since cars kill one pedestrian a day in New York, the cyclists argued that they were saving lives by encouraging people to use a different method of transport. The case is one example of how strongly people feel about cars in cities.

There are about 800 million bicycles in the world, most of which are in Asia, especially China. The bikes in Asia transport more people than all the world's cars put together. In Britain, 75 per cent of all car journeys are less than 8 km – a distance which most people could cycle. Cycles are very energy efficient – a better use of energy even than walking. And in the space taken up by one moving car about 30 bikes can travel.

In Groningen, the sixth largest city in Holland, bicycles are very important. Some 15 years ago, city centre motorways were dug up in favour of green spaces, bicycle lanes and pedestrians. More than half the citizens travel around by bike.

The city is now a quieter, safer place and more people are drawn to it. By law, all new buildings must have cycle garages. Cars must take long detours to get around the city centre and parking is difficult.

Many cities are linking stretches of paths along rivers, canals or old train tracks for walkers and cyclists. In the USA, these 'greenways' in Washington DC and Seattle are the major routes for cyclists going to work. About 500 new greenways are being built in US cities. In Britain there are 400 km of greenways – the oldest links the cities of Bath and Bristol and carries one million journeys a year.

About 18 bicycles can be parked in the space taken up by one car.

Bikes as well as buses are given priority in Copenhagen's traffic system.

To help you understand the problems of traffic and conservation you and your friends can act out the parts of people involved in a road building issue. Traffic to the motorway has increased greatly – the road through the middle of the town has become busy and dangerous. Pressure grows for a by-pass to be built around the town. There are two possible routes: **A** would pass through a housing estate; **B** would destroy an old wood. Act out the following parts and debate the issues:

A protestor who wants to save the old wood and its rare plants and animals.

A cyclist who has been hurt by a lorry in the town and wants a by-pass.

A shop owner who wants to keep traffic – and trade – in the town.

The owner of a house on the new estate threatened by route A.

A town official who wants to spend the least money on the by-pass – and use the savings to build a school.

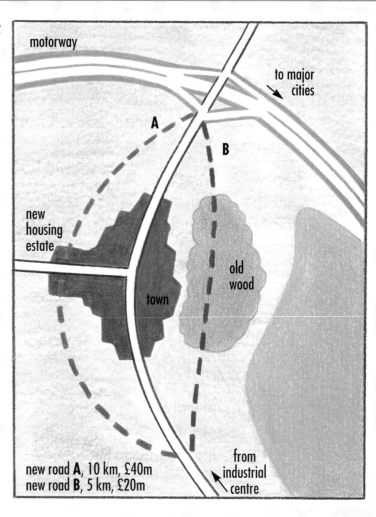

motorway

to major cities

A

B

new housing estate

old wood

town

new road **A**, 10 km, £40m
new road **B**, 5 km, £20m

from industrial centre

Planning for life

How may we make cities less polluting and less wasteful of the Earth's resources?

In rich, industrial countries, transport produces one-third of the main greenhouse gas, carbon dioxide. Even more traffic is expected to clog the roads in the years ahead. Indeed the number of cars on British roads may double within 20 years.

The way a town is planned influences the way we travel. Cities in the USA often have large suburbs with one-third fewer people per hectare than older European cities. As a result, Americans use five times as much petrol as Europeans. In Europe cities are compact enough for 1 in 5 people to journey to work on foot. In cities in the USA and Australia only 1 in every 20 journeys is on foot. Supermarkets and even hospitals are now often built on the outskirts of towns where land is cheaper than in the centre. People sometimes have to drive up to 30 km just to buy their groceries. If cities were more compact, people would not need to use their cars as much, if at all. Cities in Europe are now reducing the number of out-of-town supermarkets, and some are encouraging the building of homes, shops and offices together along the routes of public transport. Because, on average, about 5 per cent of a city is rebuilt and changed every 10 years, it may not take too long for the new planning to make a difference.

The best way to reduce traffic and pollution is to stop travelling! Millions of people around the world are now 'teleworking' from home. For these people their work place is their home – computers connect them through phone lines to a central office in the next town, or even the next country. In the USA about 27 million of the 126 million people who work have teleworked at some time.

One of the 1·25 million teleworkers in the UK.

Houses, offices and a cricket ground close together in Singapore.

Faced with the dangers of climate change, some 14 cities in Europe and North America began the 'Urban Carbon Dioxide Project' in 1991. They plan to share ideas on how to cut down the greenhouse gases made in their cities by up to a quarter by the year 2005.

From Toronto in Canada to Copenhagen in Denmark, cities will be insulating buildings, improving public transport, introducing combined heat and power stations, and many other projects. Toronto has agreed to stop its sprawl and to build new homes nearer to where the jobs are. Even though Toronto expects its population to grow, city officials intend to cut carbon dioxide creation by 20 per cent by the end of the century and to pay for the planting of new forests in South America which will soak up carbon dioxide as they grow.

Denmark's capital, Copenhagen, plans to cut its carbon dioxide production by at least 25 per cent before the end of the century.

Building for life

Towns and cities can slowly be re-planned and transport improved to make them better for the environment. Each new building, too, can do its bit! Milton Keynes claims to be Britain's most energy-efficient town. Its 'energy park' has 600 houses which have fuel bills one-third lower than the average city house. There are houses partly buried in the earth to stop heat loss, and others have one huge sloping wall made of glass to make the most of the sun's heat.

In Schiedam, a town in The Netherlands, even more energy is saved. Since 1979, all new houses have been very energy efficient. They have large windows facing the sun, and small windows which face away to reduce heat loss. All walls and roofs are fully insulated and as well as double-glazing, there are shutters made of foam to insulate the windows even more. The old houses in the town have also been double-glazed and draught-proofed.

In the newest Schiedam houses, central heating is not necessary – a water heater provides all the warmth that is needed. A pump brings in fresh air to the house and blows old stale air out. Before the old air is gone, however, a machine takes most of its heat to warm up the cold incoming air. Some of these new houses have heating bills 90 per cent lower than a normal house.

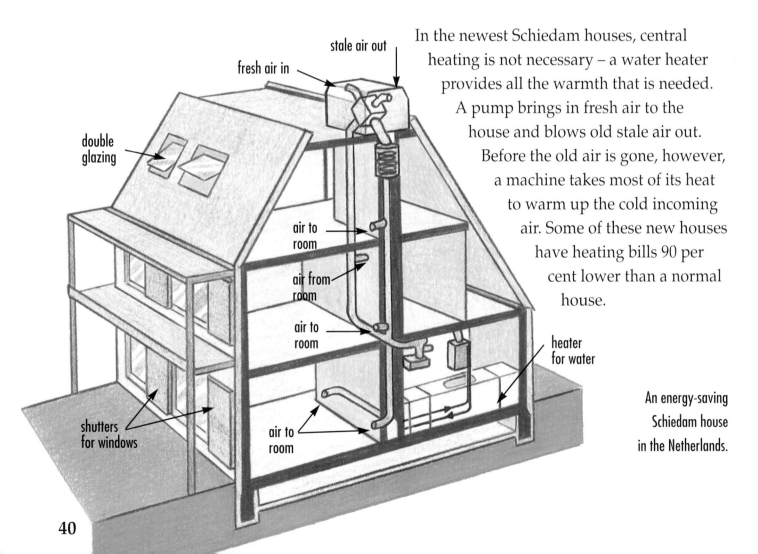

stale air out

fresh air in

double glazing

air to room

air from room

air to room

shutters for windows

air to room

heater for water

An energy-saving Schiedam house in the Netherlands.

Davis in California, USA, is a town of 44,000 people – the authorities have agreed to stop the town growing when it reaches 50,000 people. All housing is built to strict standards to save energy and 20,000 trees have been planted to shade the buildings and so reduce the need for air-conditioning to keep the homes cool. The number of houses per hectare is higher than in similar towns elsewhere in the USA. Davis has 70 km of bike lanes for 40,000 bikes – and just 9,000 cars. The town hopes to get half its energy from the sun by the year 2000.

Already solar panels to warm water are a familiar sight on roofs. People are also encouraged to grow food. Those without a garden are allowed an allotment. Fruit and vegetables are grown and sold in a twice-weekly market. Davis also has one of the best recycling systems in the USA – most people sort their rubbish into separate bins for collection. Experts in town planning from all over the USA visit Davis to study their achievements.

Typical houses in Davis, California.

Food in cities

Even if cities can be redesigned to use less energy, people still need food. Huge amounts of energy are needed to grow and then process food and transport it to the cities. This energy mostly comes from burning oil which will not be easily available forever. Up to a third of fresh fruit and vegetables spoil in transit and must be dumped by the time they reach the cities. But could food be grown in cities?

It has been done before. In the 1930s, in a time when many people were poor and out of work, there were 5,000 food gardens in New York City. Ten years later during World War II, 'Victory Gardens' grew about 40 per cent of all the USA's vegetables; 1·5 million plots in the UK covered 57,000 hectares. Even today, there are half a million allotments in Britain which are mostly used for vegetables. In the USA, 2 million city gardeners tend food plots and greenhouses.

Throughout western Europe there are more than 1,000 'city farms'. London has 17 of these farms, and in Britain's second city, Birmingham, derelict land is converted to vegetable gardens at Ashram Acres. The local people rarely get the chance to visit the countryside, but here they can see how their food is grown. People who came to

Sunny balconies are splendid for growing plants.

Birmingham from farming regions in Pakistan, India and the Caribbean use their farming skills to grow the food. There are 800 'community gardens' in New York City providing food for the farmers' markets which are visited by 50,000 New Yorkers every week. One scientist has even suggested turning 10 per cent of New York's rooftops into greenhouse gardens to grow all the city's vegetables.

Air pollution is a major problem for city food growers. But because the worst pollution tends to stay near the ground, balconies and window boxes may not be badly affected. Likewise backyards separated from the road escape many of the fumes. Trees or shrubs growing around food plots also filter out much pollution.

A roof top garden in Nepal provides vegetables for the family.

MAKE A FOOD CONTAINER GARDEN

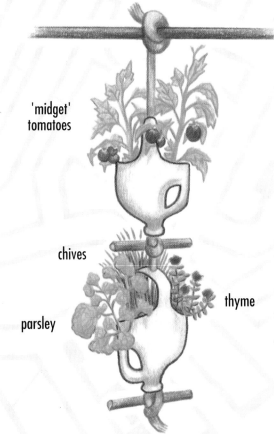

'midget' tomatoes

chives

parsley

thyme

A hanging garden.

You can grow food anywhere – on balconies, window ledges, stairs. Choose a good place facing the sun if possible. Light-weight plastic pots or tubs are best and old buckets or cut up plastic bottles can be attached to hangers.

Put a few centimetres of gravel in the bottom of your container and add soil or compost. Try planting 'midget' varieties of foods like tomatoes, as well as strawberries and gooseberries. Sow the seeds and cover with a little soil. Grow two or more varieties of plants together, such as lettuce, radishes and carrots – they need as little as 12 cm of soil. Water your plants regularly.

If you live near a busy road, don't grow leafy vegetables as these collect the dirt.

The sustainable city

To be sustainable, cities must meet their needs in ways which do not damage the environment so much that their needs – and their people's needs – cannot be met in the future.

Every day London uses up the energy contained in one supertanker of oil, eats 7,600 tonnes of food and gives out 37,000 tonnes of solid waste and 164,000 tonnes of carbon dioxide. Cities are not 'sustainable'; they are leaving the world more polluted for the next generation of people.

Try to imagine a city of the future that is sustainable and cares for the environment. Such a city may not be the science-fiction idea of massive skyscrapers sprawling as far as the eye can see. It is perhaps more likely that city centres will be compact, and that buildings and neighbourhoods will generate their own power. More people will work at home or very near their home – and may not even have to live in a large city to do their job. Buses and trains will carry people around town and when cars are needed, electric vehicles and cars powered by non-polluting fuels will be used. With less pollution, it would be possible to grow far more food in and around cities – on derelict land, or even on rooftops. And this could be fertilized by waste from the city.

In the city of Curitiba in Brazil and the town of Davis in California we can see something of the future. Although many of Curitiba's citizens are poor – and their main worry each day is getting enough food to eat – almost everyone does their bit to help make their city sustainable. Even the people in the shanty towns sort their rubbish for recycling and put out their waste in plastic bags. If a city with as many problems as Curitiba can become more sustainable, so the cities of the rich world surely can follow the example.

Cities of the future – some computer software allows you to design your own sustainable city. This design was produced by the program Sim City 2000.

DID YOU KNOW?

Green cities

Greenery is also making a comeback in cities; people seem to need nature in their surroundings. In the last 15 years, Paris has increased the amount of its green space by half. New York City has probably the greatest variety of nature of any city in its 85,000 hectares of parks and 2·6 million street trees. We are realising that cities, after all, are part of nature. If we are serious about saving the Earth, our cities may be the best places to start.

Biosphere II in the Arizona desert, USA – an attempt to recreate the ecology of the Earth and find out how space colonies could recycle their waste, water and air. Teams of 8 people are sealed in it for two years at a time, but have to be supplied with electricity, and extra food and air.

Glossary

Acid rain Rain is normally slightly acid. Yet the gases released from the burning of fuels such as coal can combine with the water in the air to give damaging acid rain.

CHP Combined Heat and Power. A power station that generates electricity and also supplies its 'waste' heat to a town.

Developing countries The poorer nations of the world which are becoming industrial. Most are in Africa, South America and Asia.

Ecology The study of how living things affect each other, and how they are affected by their environment.

Environment Everything, both living and non-living, that surrounds and affects a life form.

Fossil fuels Coal, oil and natural gas, which were created millions of years ago from the remains of once-living life forms.

Greenhouse gases Some gases, such as carbon dioxide, trap heat energy in the Earth's atmosphere. This is how the Earth stays at the kind of temperature that can support life. Since the Industrial Revolution the amounts of greenhouse gases released into the air have been increasing and so has the average temperature of the atmosphere.

Greenway A path or track made especially for walkers and cyclists.

Industrial Revolution A time 100-200 years ago when the countries of Europe and North America changed from nations whose wealth was based on farming into nations whose wealth is based on industry.

Pollution The release of substances, known as pollutants, into the air, water or land which may upset the natural balance of the environment.

Rain forests The dense, evergreen forests found in some of the tropical areas of the world.

Renaissance A period in the fifteenth and sixteenth centuries of great learning and achievements in the arts and sciences. It began in Italy and spread northward across Europe.

Sewage A mixture of waste and water that is carried from buildings in underground pipes called sewers.

Smog A harmful mixture of moisture, smoke and gases that may form in the air over towns.

Solar cell A device which can convert the sun's energy into electricity.

Species The name given to the smallest grouping or 'type' of plant and animal. There are believed to be about 30 million different species on the Earth.

Teleworking Working from home on a computer connected to a phone line.

Resources

Organizations to contact

United Kingdom
British Waste Paper Association
Station Road, Aldershot
Hants GU11 1BQ

Centre for Alternative Technology
Machynlleth, Powys
Wales, SY20 9AZ

Centre of the Earth
42 Norman Street, Winson Green
Birmingham B18 7EP

Council for Environmental Education
University of Reading
Reading RG1 5AQ

Friends of the Earth
26-28 Underwood Street
London N1 7JQ

Global Action Plan
42 Kingsway, London WC2B

Greenpeace
Canonbury Villas, London N1 2PN

London Ecology Unit, Bedford House
125 Camden High Street
London NW1 7JR

Tidy Britain Group, The Pier
Wigan WN3 4EX

Transport 2000, Walkden House
10 Melton Street, London NW1 2EJ

Trust for Urban Ecology
PO Box 514, London SE16 1AS

Waste Watch, 68 Grafton Way
London W1P 5LE

Australia
Australian Association for
Environmental Education
GPO Box 112, Canberra, ACT 2601

Australian Conservation Foundation
340 Gore Street, Fitzroy, VIC 3065

Clean Up the World
123 Harris Street, Pymont
Sydney, NSW 2009

Friends of the Earth
PO Box 530E, Melbourne, VIC 3001

Canada
Friends of the Earth
251 Laurier Avenue W, Suite 701
Ottawa, Ontario K1P 5J6

International Council for Local
Environmental Initiatives
City Hall, East Tower, 8th Floor
Toronto, Ontario M5H 2N2

New Zealand
Environment and Conservation
Organizations of New Zealand
PO Box 11057, Wellington

Friends of the Earth, PO Box 39-065
Auckland-West

Books to read

Stephen Croall and William Rankin,
Ecology for Beginners, Icon Books, 1993
The Earth Works Group, *50 Simple
Things Kids Can Do to Save the Earth*,
Sphere, 1990
Fala Favela, CAFOD, 1992
Friends of the Earth, *Going Green at
Home and School*, Wayland, 1993
Barbara James, *Recycling*,
Wayland, 1990
Aileen Mackenzie, *City Lights*,
WWF, 1991
Nairobi: Kenyan City Life,
Action Aid, 1992
Norman Myers (ed), *The Gaia Atlas of
Planet Management*, Gaia, 1994
Philip Parker, *Water for Life*,
Simon & Schuster, 1990
Prue Poulton & Gillian Symons,
Eco School, WWF UK, 1993
Right Up Your Street, Friends of
the Earth, 1992
Tony Reynolds, *Cities in Crisis*,
Wayland, 1989
David Wright, *Environmental Atlas*,
George Philip, 1992
WWF/Birmingham DEC, *A Tale of
Two Cities*, WWF UK, 1991
WWF/Birmingham DEC, *Where We
Live*, WWF UK, 1989

Videos/software/multimedia
Only One Earth, WWF/North-South
Productions, 1989 (video pack)
SATCOM, WWF, 1991
SimCity 2000, Maxis, 1994

Index